A Victorian Christmas Coloring Book

Color in the Nostalgic Traditions of Yule Times Past

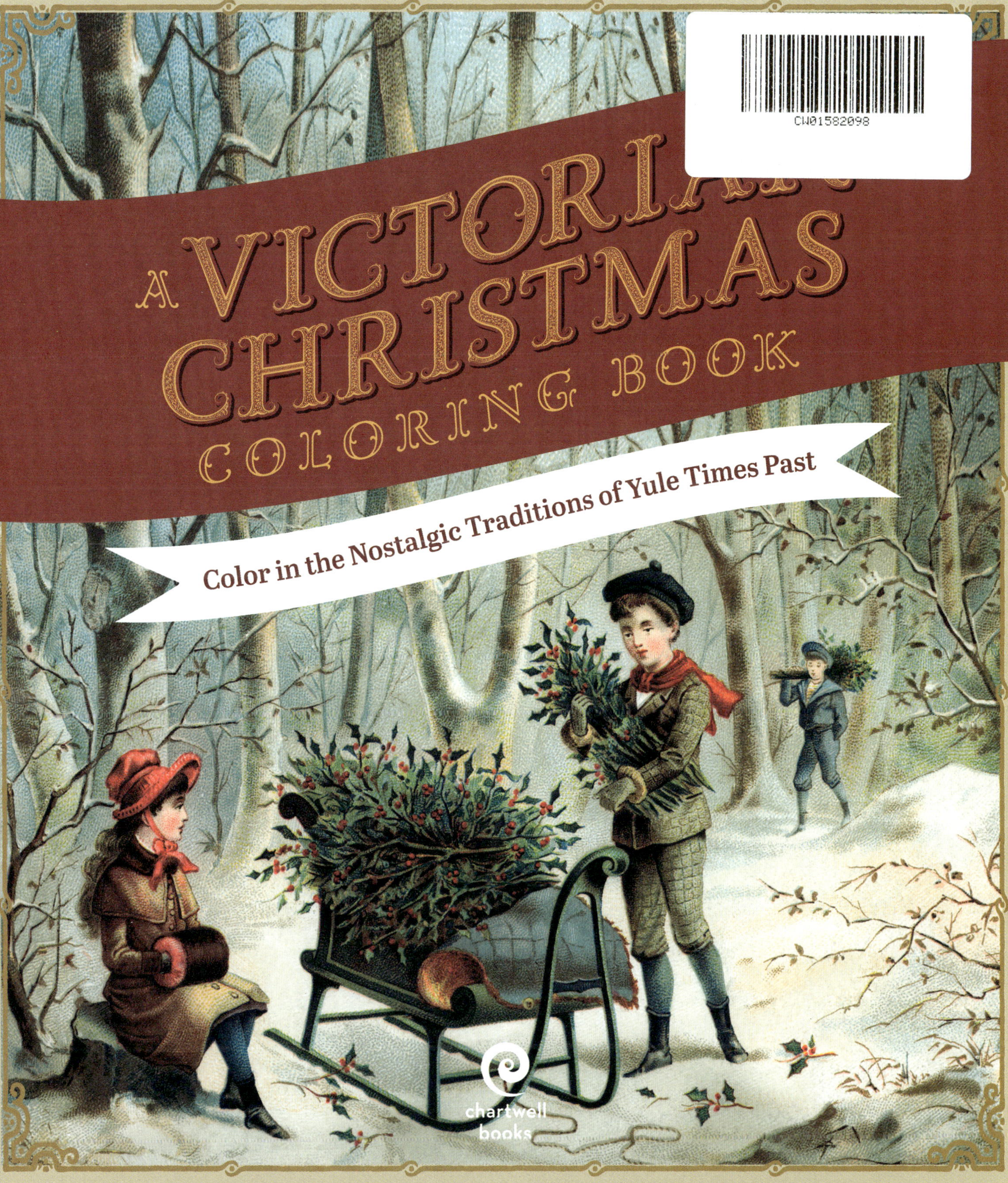

chartwell books

From presents to Christmas puddings, color in the favorite Christmas traditions from the 19th century.

Many of Victorian England's traditions will seem familiar to us. Our ideas of what Christmas is today can be traced to the reign of Queen Victoria and her own ideas of the holiday. As the British Empire grew, Christmas became a blend of different cultures around western Europe and North America, creating the "typical," nostalgic Christmas that we recognize.

One very important symbol was thought to have been introduced by Victoria's husband, Prince Albert. Inspired by his German heritage, he imported several spruce firs from Germany in 1840; they were brought indoors and adorned with lit candles and other trinkets. (It was, however, Queen Charlotte, the German wife of George III, who actually put up the first known Christmas tree in England 40 years earlier.) The custom caught on a few years after Albert first imported the trees, when periodicals began depicting the royals at Christmas. By 1860, the trees were popular in middle class homes as well, covered with candles, sweets, fruit, homemade decorations, and small gifts. The Queen continued these festive traditions after the prince's death in 1861 as a way of keeping his memory alive, inspiring a nation to do the same.

In addition to the indoor tree, the rest of the home was filled with evergreen decorations. Holly and fir garlands were strewn on mantelpieces. Known as "welcome rings," wreaths made of holly, ivy, pinecones, and ribbons, were hung on front doors. Though not invented by the Victorians, the advent wreath was first recorded in England in

1833, when a Lutheran clergyman lit a candle in a wreath every Sunday in December and told the nativity story.

Around the time of the Christmas tree, the first-ever Christmas card was created in 1843 by Sir Henry Cole, who would become the first director of the Victoria and Albert Museum. The cards caught on, with typical depictions of the time, including robins, kittens, angels, wintery scenes, festive feasts, Christmas trees, mistletoe, and by 1870, Father Christmas.

The image of Father Christmas was still evolving. Sometimes he was depicted in his now-trademark red cloak, hat, and long white beard, but other times he was more mischievous and hooded. He was always portrayed as a jolly fellow, presiding over feasts, gift giving, and general merriment.

Though the Victorians did not introduce the tradition of Christmas presents, they did make it a part of their family festivities, sharing them on Christmas Eve, rather than Christmas Day. In Queen Victoria's home, unwrapped presents were spread out across tables (a tradition stemming from royal birthdays). The Queen gave gifts of gratitude to her 100+ servants, an act so important to her that she did it before she and her family opened their own presents.

You can encounter some of these traditions, and many more, in the nostalgic pages that follow. Take time for yourself out of your own bustling holiday activities, and relax while you color in the designs and images however you like. Or share them with your family and make your own holiday tradition. This is a time for celebration and enjoyment. Happy Christmas!

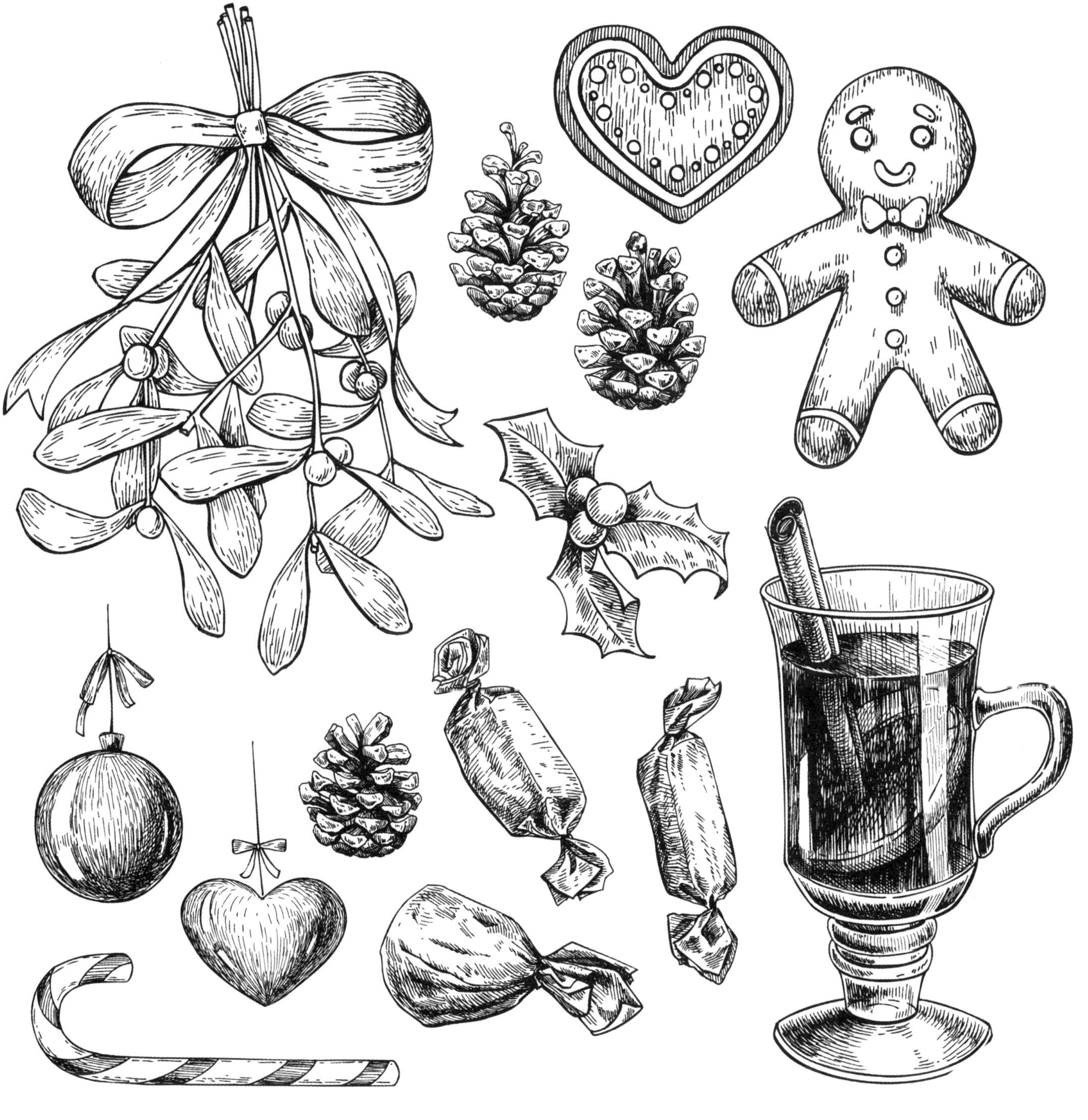

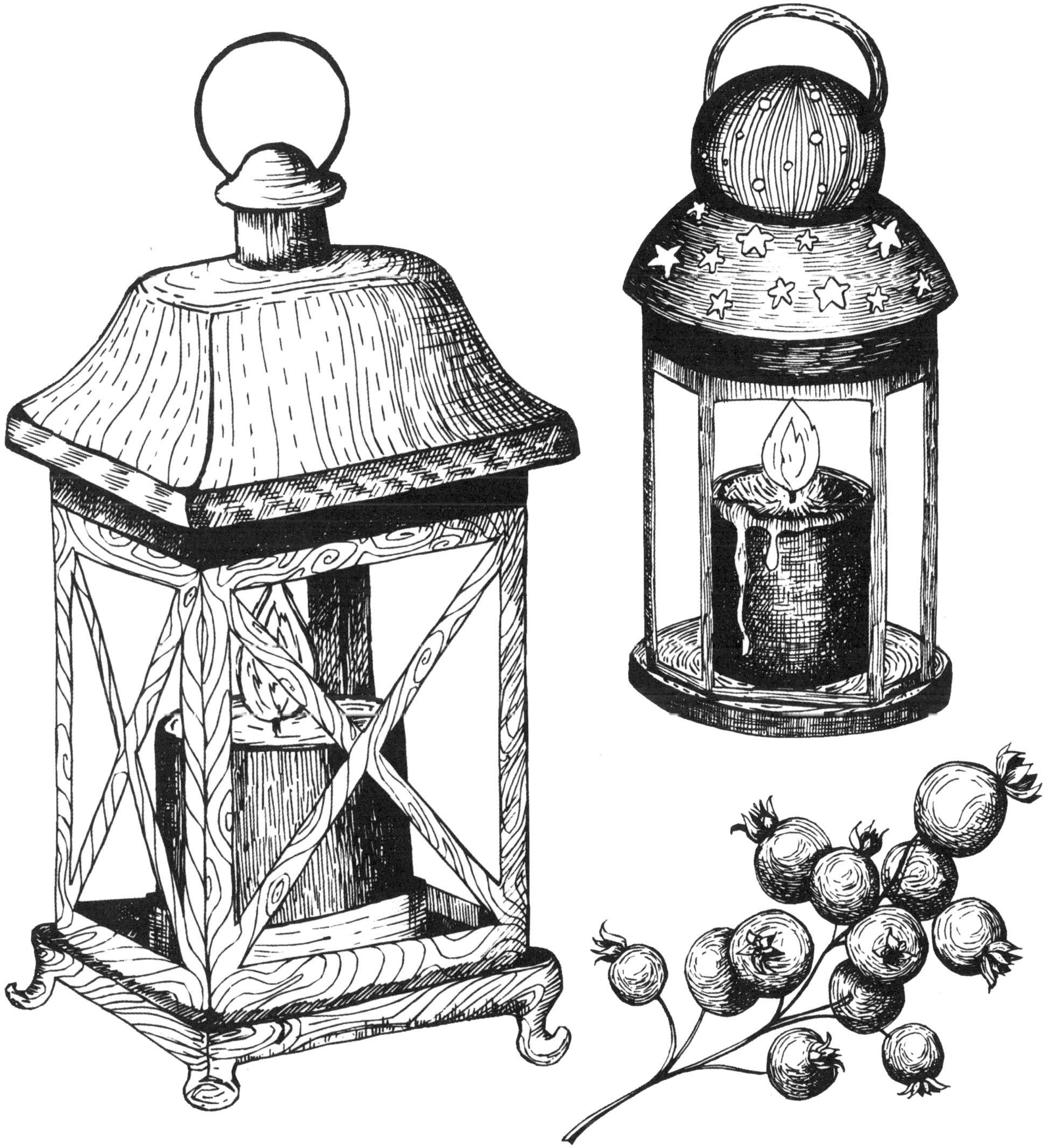

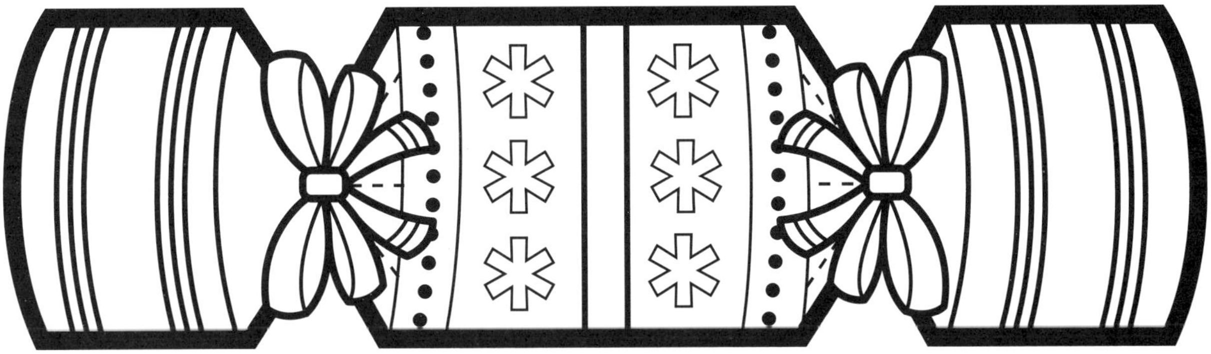

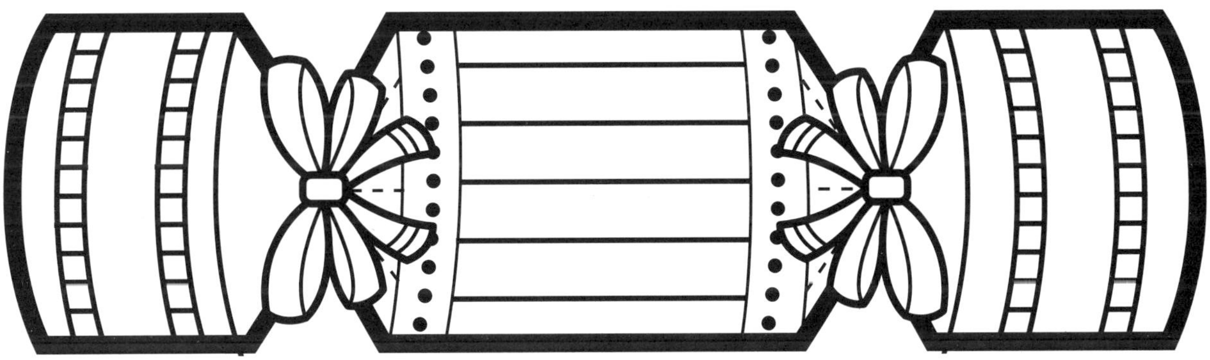

IX
III
VI

Quarto

This edition published in 2024 by Chartwell Books,
an imprint of The Quarto Group
142 West 36th Street, 4th Floor
New York, NY 10018 USA
T (212) 779-4972 F (212) 779-6058
www.Quarto.com

10 9 8 7 6 5 4 3 2 1

Chartwell titles are also available at discount for retail, wholesale, promotional, and bulk purchase. For details, contact the Special Sales Manager by email at special-sales@quarto.com or by mail at The Quarto Group, Attn: Special Sales Manager, 100 Cummings Center Suite 265D, Beverly, MA 01915, USA.

ISBN: 978-0-7858-4538-6

Publisher: Wendy Friedman
Senior Publishing Manager: Meredith Mennitt
Cover Designer: Angelika Piwowarczyk
Designer: Susan Boylan
Editor: Jennifer Kushnier
Image credits: Shutterstock

Printed in China